THE FOUNDING
OF A NATION

THE FOUNDING
OF A NATION
THE STORY OF THE 13 COLONIES

by ELIZABETH RICHARDS

TATE PUBLISHING & *Enterprises*

Published by Tate Publishing & Enterprises, LLC
127 E. Trade Center Terrace | Mustang, Oklahoma 73064 USA
1.888.361.9473 | www.tatepublishing.com

Tate Publishing is committed to excellence in the publishing industry. The company reflects the philosophy established by the founders, based on Psalm 68:11,
"The Lord gave the word and great was the company of those who published it."

Book design copyright © 2008 by Tate Publishing, LLC. All rights reserved.
Cover design by Jacob Crissup
Interior design by Jonathan Lindsey
Illustration by Lisa Hubbell
Published in the United States of America

ISBN: 978-1-60604-345-5
1. Education: History   2. History:US:Col.Per./Rev.War
08.07.21

Dedication

This booklet is dedicated to my seven grandchildren in the order of their arrival in the family: Michael, Rain, Merrick, Lane, Isabella, Mason, and finally, my newest granddaughter, Whitney.

Elizabeth Richards
Walnut Creek, CA
September 2007

Acknowledgements

History has been my love since high school even though it was sometimes taught in a very uninteresting way. Notwithstanding that problem, there was always something about the subject that held my interest.

The first person I want to thank is my first history professor at Wilson (Professor Miller) who made the subject so fascinating for me. I also must thank my two children who patiently listened to me as I constantly tried to teach them history while they were growing up. Thank you, Michael and Jennifer, for at least feigning interest while I rattled on with my stories, which I hope were somewhat interesting to both of you.

Next in the order of thanks goes to my oldest two grand children, Michael and Rain, who mentioned, within my hearing, something so completely incorrect about American history that I felt compelled to begin writing my books to correct their misinformation.

So much of history is not taught any longer, and students are graduating from high school with no knowledge of how this country was founded, what the Founders created in the writing of our Constitution, and sadly many don't know why we celebrate the 4th of July. A *Man on the Street* interview last July on Sean Hannity's New York radio program asked people at random what is the meaning of July 4, and none of the people interviewed could answer that it was our Independence Day. I think that is a national disgrace.

I also must thank my sister, Barbara, who after reading my books made suggestions for changes and encouraged me to look for a publisher for my books. Thank you, Barbara. I also want to thank my friend Doris, who patiently re-read my writings and made suggestions of how to make certain parts clearer. Doris also caught more than one typo in my chapters. Thank you to Doris.

Last but not least, to my friend Lisa, whose beautiful drawings became an essential part of this book. Lisa, your artwork is truly inspirational, and I thank you for taking the time to create the artwork for this book.

If I have forgotten to name anybody, my apologies to you. The oversight was unintentional.

Elizabeth Richards

Contents

MAPS

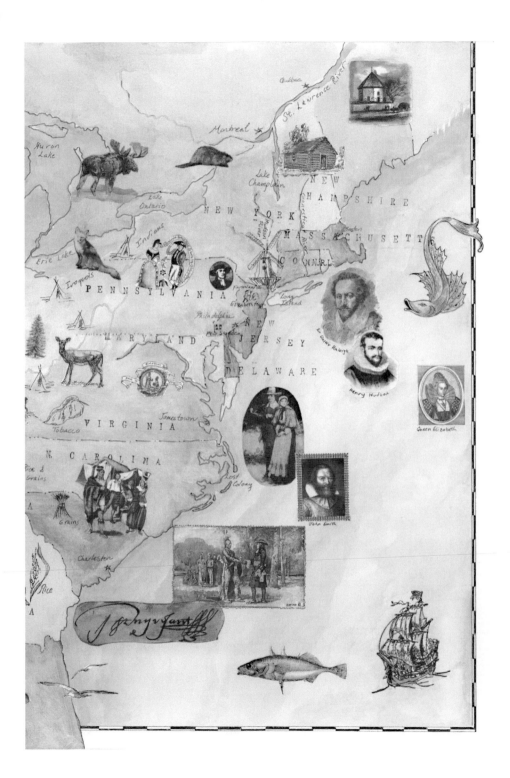

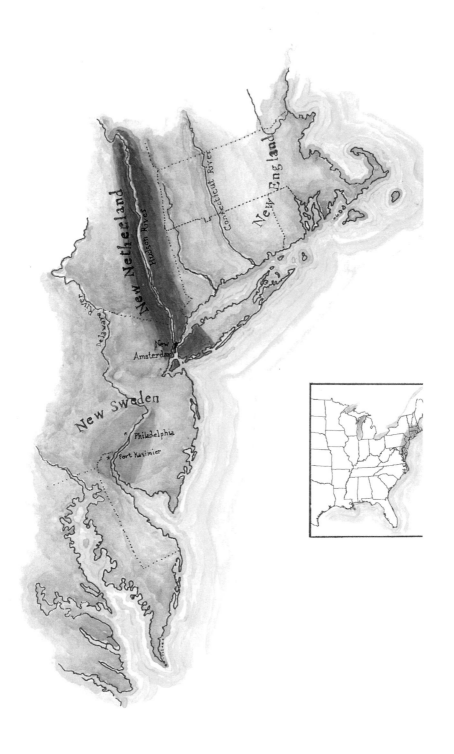

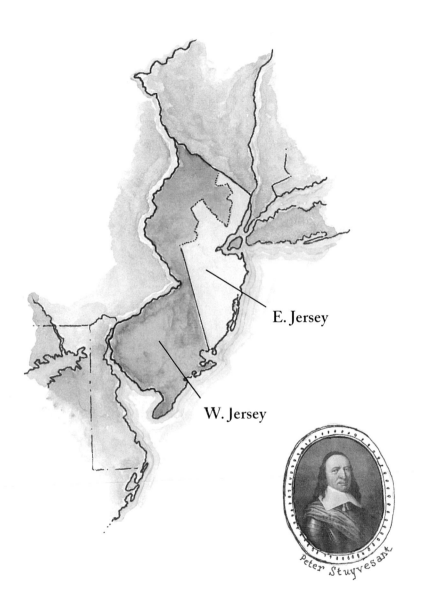

E. Jersey

W. Jersey

Peter Stuyvesant

Introduction

Understanding who we are as a people, how we began, and where we are going as a country is essential for young people today to know. You cannot understand history by looking at it through your twenty-first-century eyes. You can only understand it by looking at the period of time just before the particular event being discussed.

Migrations of people have occurred since the dawn of time. People migrated; tribes migrated, usually from east to west, but not always that way. As an example, around the year 476 AD there was a mass migration of different tribes—the Huns, the Slavs, the Goths, the Visagoths and others tribes that migrated and broke down the mighty Roman Empire.

During the Roman period, the climate of Europe, including England and Scotland, was much warmer than it is today. There is speculation that these northern tribes began to migrate because the weather was turning colder (Europe suffered a mini ice age in the Middle Ages), and perhaps that is what caused these tribes to move south and west to get to a warmer climate. We don't know the reasons because these tribes left no written records, but we do know that huge migrations took place.

The years between the 1300s and 1500s are called the Age of Discovery. Up until this time, people believed the world was flat, and it was feared that if you sailed past the horizon you would fall off the face of the earth. These early explorers sailed west, and when they returned they proved that they didn't fall off the earth; in fact, they learned that the earth was not flat at all, but round.

These explorers brought back tales of newly-discovered lands with different vegetation than what was known in Europe and peopled with natives they called Indians. The countries of Holland (the Dutch), Spain, England, Portugal, and France all sent explorers to visit these new lands and claim the lands for their respective kings or queens. In fact, what they did is say this new land was an extension of England, Holland, Spain, Portugal, and France. It was a time of flux in the world. No country wanted to be outdone by another country, and each scrambled to claim more land than another country.

When gold and silver were discovered in what became Mexico, South and Central America, Spain conquered these lands and enslaved the native population to work in its mines; the riches were sent back to Spain. Spain also claimed parts of our southwest, but no gold or silver was discovered there, so Spain concentrated on its holding in Mexico, South America and Central America.

France set up trading posts in what are now Canada and the central part of our country to establish a fur trade with the Indians. These furs were sent back to France for sale. During this time, England, Sweden, and the Dutch claimed different parts of the eastern coast of North America.

The English king or queen issued charters to different trading companies that would in turn get settlers to go to the colonies. The purpose of establishing these colonies was to make money for the trading companies and in turn make money for England. The Virginia Company held the charter for the particular part of the North American coast that became the Virginia Colony. The Virginia Company hoped its settlers would be successful in finding gold or silver that would enrich the stockholders, as well as England, but no gold or silver was found in the Virginia Colony.

The English Colonies in North America were different than the colonies set up by any other country, and we can be grateful that England prevailed in becoming the country that established the thirteen colonies, because the formation of our country was a unique happening in the history of the world. After the Revolutionary War, when we broke away from England, learned men sat down and wrote a constitution upon which a brand new country was to be formed. It was a grand experiment that had never happened in the history of the world before that time. Other countries evolved into the present countries they are, but here people came together, argued, and wrote a constitution for all peoples, and it has endured for more than two hundred years. In no other country in the world do a people enjoy as many freedoms as we do.

The story of our country really began way back in the history of England in the year 1215 when King John of England was forced, by some of his barons, to sign a document called the Magna Carta. This document, among other things, prevented the king from taxing the barons without their consent. King John had driven England nearly to bankruptcy because he spent so much money to fund his continual participation in the Crusades (the Crusades were a period in history when Christian knights tried to re-take the Holy Land, which had been conquered by the Muslims). The barons were tired of being taxed to pay for his wars. This document was essentially a document in medieval times to clarify the differences between the three powers in England at the time—the Catholic Church, the king, and the barons.

This is an important document, because it was the first time in history that people other than the king or the church were given some powers. It did nothing about granting rights to the peasants and the merchant class. This is important because it was the very first time in the history of the world that the king and the church had their powers curbed. Not one other country in the world at this time had a Magna Carta (many still don't), and this is important because it was the English who were the first ones to colonize the areas of our country, which was first known as the thirteen colonies. These colonists brought with them these truly revolutionary ideas of individual freedom.

I have felt compelled to write the story of the founding of this country beginning with the story of the thirteen colonies, because I feel history is not taught adequately in the schools today, and entire generations of American children are growing up without any knowledge of the "Grand Experiment," that was the beginning of this nation.

Our winning the Revolutionary War, which gave us our independence from England, was a miracle in itself, then the writing of the Constitution and the early years of this nation, as men worked out how we were going to operate as a country, became the miraculous events that created this new country. This book is the first of five books that tell the story of our history, from the founding of the thirteen colonies through the presidency of Teddy Roosevelt.

Yes, I know women were not able to vote when the Constitution was written, but nowhere in the world did women have the right to vote at that time. Yes, this country had a dark period in which there was slavery, but we did not create the system of slavery; it was already in existence, and the colonies, mostly the southern colonies, made use of it. As far back as biblical times there were slaves. Usually when a country was defeated in a war, the survivors were sold into slavery; it was something that happened again and again throughout the history of the world. Again, it was a bad period in the history of our country, but we got rid of slavery in this country. Unfortunately, today there are still slave traders in existence; the Arab nations are among those who continue to trade in slaves.

We were often not good neighbors to our Indian neighbors, but the original settlers did purchase the land from the Indians; they didn't steal it. It was later in our history, however, that the Indian policy was detrimental to the Indian nations. That was a period in our history, like the period of slavery, that was not handled the way it should have been. It is important to note that we as a nation have consistently tried to better the lives of our citizens and make amends for past injustices. When we look at these "dark" periods in our history, you should look at them not with twenty-first-century eyes, but eighteenth and nineteenth-century eyes. That is the only way to understand how and why these things happened and how later we made changes to the system.

This is not a perfect nation, but it is the best one so far created by man. I hope that by reading these stories you will be inspired to learn more about the founding of our great nation.

One last thing you need to become aware of is that it takes a certain type of personality of men and women to leave a known world to trek across an ocean and settle in a new land, while often facing hostile weather and hostile Indians. Some came because they were not the oldest sons and would not inherit the land or the family business in England or other countries; others came because they were felons and were offered banishment in lieu of death or residing in the gaol (an English jail). Some came for religious freedoms, and some others came hoping to make a fortune in trade. Each for his own reason, but mostly, all who came showed an incredible amount of inner strength and determination that allowed them to survive and prosper in ways undreamed about in the old country. This then is the story of our ancestors who came to this country, and because they did, you, their descendants, now have a better life and freedoms still not available to many people in other parts of the world.

You can take all our freedoms for granted, or you can take charge and make sure that never again will a government control the personal lives of its citizens. It is up to each of you to take upon yourselves to become informed citizens and to preserve these freedoms for your children and grandchildren. It is up to you; learn all you can about our history so that you are the catalyst to preventing our freedoms from evaporating.

Elizabeth Richards

December 2007

The Thirteen Colonies in Order of Settlement:

- **The Lost Colony**—attempted colonization in 1584–1587, none successful;
- **Virginia**—founded by London Company in 1607, became a Royal Colony in 1624;
- **Massachusetts**—founded in 1620 by Puritans, became a Royal Colony in 1691;
- **Maryland**—founded in 1634 by Lord Baltimore;
- **Connecticut**—founded in 1635 by Thomas Hooker;
- **Rhode Island**—founded in 1634 by Roger Williams;
- **Delaware**—founded in 1638 by Peter Minuit and the New Sweden Company;
- **New Hampshire**—founded in 1638 by John Wheelwright, became a Royal Colony in 1679;
- **North Carolina**—founded in 1653 by the Virginians, became a Royal Colony in 1729;
- **South Carolina**—founded in 1663 by eight nobles with a Royal charter from Charles II, became a Royal Colony in 1729;
- **New Jersey**—founded in 1664 by Lord Berkeley and Sir George Carteret, became a Royal Colony in 1702;

- **New York**—founded in 1664 by the Duke of York, became a Royal Colony in 1685;
- **Pennsylvania**—founded in 1682 by William Penn;
- **Georgia**—founded in 1732 by James Edward Oglethorpe, became a Royal Colony in 1752.

Roanoke Island, the Lost Colony

There were three attempts to found a colony on Roanoke Island, and none of them succeeded. Roanoke Island is located off the coast of what today is North Carolina, but at the time of the attempted founding, the area was called Virginia.

In the year 1584 two explorers, Philip Amadas and Arthur Barlows, were the first to see Roanoke Island; they had been sent by Sir Walter Raleigh to search for an ideal location for an English settlement. The two explorers returned to England with glowing reports of the island, which was full of abundant wild life and lovely oak trees. Queen Elizabeth I was pleased with what they found and gave a patent to Sir Walter Raleigh to all the lands he could occupy. The new land was named "Virginia" in honor of Queen Elizabeth I because she was known as the virgin (unmarried) queen.

The first attempt to settle the island occurred in 1584 when one hundred soldiers, craftsmen, and scholars were sent to Roanoke Island to form the colony. Unfortunately, this settlement was doomed to failure because they arrived too late in the year to plant crops before the winter set in, and the supplies they brought with them ran out. The scholars were "gentlemen" who were not used to having to work for a living and were ill-suited to the task of creating a colony in the wilderness. Their situation was made worse because their captain, Captain Lane, alienated the neighboring Roanoke Indians by murdering their chief whom the settlers accused of stealing a cup. The Indians had been supplying food for the colonists, but with the murder of their chief, they stopped giving the settlers food.

The second attempt at founding a settlement occurred in 1586 when Sir Francis Drake stopped at Roanoke and found Captain Lane and his men were starving. They abandoned the settlement and returned to England with Sir Francis Drake. A week later a supply ship from England arrived; they found the island deserted. It was decided by the captain of the supply ship to leave fifteen men on the island to maintain the fort until reinforcements could be brought from England.

The third attempt to settle the colony came when Sir Walter Raleigh, who was still determined to form a permanent colony on the island, arrived with another group of settlers to augment the settlement. The 117 new settlers reached the island in the spring of 1587. When they arrived they found the fort deserted and the fifteen men murdered by the Indians.

The three most important names of those settlers were John White, who was appointed governor of the island, his pregnant daughter Eleanor Dare, and her husband, Annanais Dare. They landed on Roanoke Island in July 1587, and on August 18, Eleanor gave birth to a daughter, and she named the baby Virginia.

With winter approaching and with their supplies running out, John White decided to return to England for supplies. He left for England in the late summer of 1587, leaving behind the settlers, including his son-in-law, daughter, and granddaughter.

Unfortunately, John White was delayed in his return to Roanoke Island for three years because of the impending invasion of England by Spain, as all available ships were needed to dispel the Spanish. The Spanish Armada (an armada is a large fleet of war ships) set off from Spain with the intention of invading England, but the armada encountered a violent storm, and the Spanish ships were destroyed. Once the invasion was repelled, John White secured a ship to return to Roanoke Island. He arrived on August 18, 1590, which was his granddaughter's third birthday, but he found the settlement deserted.

When John White left them three years earlier, he instructed them that should they have to move from the fort area they should carve a Maltese cross above the place where they had moved; there was no such cross to be found upon the island. The only clue to the disappearance of the settlers was found carved into the surface of the fort—a single word "Croatoan" and the letters "CRO" carved into a near by tree. Croatoan was the name of the Indian tribe that lived on the island south of Roanoke Island. This island today is named Hatteras.

John White was prevented from sailing to Hatteras because his ship was damaged in a hurricane on the way to Roanoke Island and the ship captain forced their return to England for repairs. John White was never able to raise the funds to return to Roanoke Island to search for his family.

What happened to the 117 people? There are several theories. One of the most plausible is: in 1709 an English explorer named John Lawson visited Roanoke Island and spent some time among the Hatteras Indians who are the descendants of the Croatoan tribe. There he found several "Indians" who had white skin and gray eyes and who could also speak English. In 1880 a man named Hamilton Macmillan, who lived near a settlement of Pembroke Indians, claimed that their ancestors came from Roanoke Island to Virginia. These Indians spoke English and had last names of many of the lost colonists. They also had European features: fair eyes, light hair, and Anglo-Saxon bone structures.

Documents found in Spanish and British archives also provide another possible solution. After John White left for England, the colonists split into two groups; one group departed for the Chesapeake Bay; the other group stayed on Roanoke Island awaiting the return of John Smith. It was this last group that possibly assimilated into the Croatoan tribe.

When the Jamestown colonists arrived in 1607, they found that (possibly) the lost colonists had been living in the area, and from the Indian chief Powhatan they learned that the colonists had been living among the friendly Chesapeake Indians. Powhatan claimed to have attacked the settlers and that most of them had been killed.[1] In any event, no real trace of them has ever been found and what really happened to them remains a mystery.

The Virginia Colony

The Virginia Colony, the first permanent colony in North America, was founded in 1607. The settlement was called Jamestown, after James I who was then king of England. Jamestown was located on a river they named the James River. The remains of the settlement can be seen today.

Jamestown was financed by the London Company, a group of London entrepreneurs who hoped to make a profit from the resources in the New World. Investors became members of the London Company by buying shares in the company or, if unable to purchase shares, a man could become an "Adventurer" and travel to Virginia to work as a "Planter." Planters were required to work for the company for a set number of years (usually three-year contracts) and in exchange were given food, clothing, and housing. At the end of their service, the Planters were to be given a piece of land to farm and would no longer be indebted to the company. If the company made a profit from the colony, the Planters were also entitled to a share of the profits.

Spain was a very powerful country at this time, and it had been increasing its wealth from the mining of gold and silver in the territories it had conquered in Central and South America. Because Spain was so rich and powerful, England felt threatened by Spain, and England, too, was eager to get gold and silver for its treasury. England is an island, and as such it could only be conquered by an army arriving by boat; England needed to build up its navy to prevent being conquered by Spain. Many of the investors in the Virginia Company hoped that the land north of the Spanish colonies would also be rich in gold and silver.

People were encouraged to immigrate to the colony, many with the hopes of gaining wealth, and those who could not afford the cost of the passage came as indentured servants to work, usually for seven years, in exchange for free passage to Virginia. Life as an indentured servant was hard; the men had no freedom during their period of service and were sometimes subject to mistreatment by their masters. Unfortunately, at times the company didn't live up to its end of the bargain, and some men were kept in servitude after they had worked the set seven years of their contract. Other masters were honorable and released their indentured servants at the end of their contracts.

In May 1607, 104 English men and boys sailed to the area of the New World known as Virginia. They selected an area on a peninsula (now called Jamestown Island) located on a river they named James River. These first settlers were all men; women didn't come to Virginia until 1619. The men expected to find gold and spent their time trying to find gold. After an attack by an Indian tribe, the men decided they had to build a fort. The settlers were unprepared for the hot summers and the very cold winters. Some of those who chose to come to Virginia were not prepared for the hard work it would entail to survive in the wilderness. Many of them who chose to come were "gentlemen-adventurers" who didn't know how to work and had no skills to enable them to survive. They were lured to Virginia with the promise of land and wealth, but most of them didn't know how to farm or hunt, and they had to rely upon the Indians for food.

The first year the settlers faced starvation and disease, and only thirty-two of the original 104 survived the first winter. Captain John Smith, who was the leader of the colony, was the only one of the colonists who was able to keep a semblance of peace between the colonists and the Indians. Because the settlers were more interested in finding gold and silver than building a fort and planting crops to feed themselves, Captain Smith needed the food the Indians provided to them for the colony to survive.

In 1608 another ship docked at Jamestown and brought new colonists and supplies. Captain John Smith knew the supplies would not last for a second winter, and he left the colony to explore the surrounding area. On his trip he traded goods made in England with the Indians in exchange for food, mostly corn.

When John Smith arrived back in Jamestown, he found most of the men were still more interested in finding gold than in growing food. John made a new rule for the colony. All men were required to work at least six hours a day either growing food or building houses for the colonists. He said, "He that will not work shall not eat."[2]

At this time the colony was still not prosperous, and the London Company was threatening to abandon the colony and the surviving colonists. John Smith, not willing to abandon the colony, sent a letter back to the London Company telling them that he needed settlers who were skilled as farmers, blacksmiths, carpenters; in other words he needed men who knew trades and how to work in order for the colony to survive.

In 1609, four hundred new colonists arrived in Jamestown. Shortly after their arrival, John Smith was hurt in a gunpowder explosion, and when the ship sailed back to England, John Smith returned to England to recover. The new leader, George Percy, was not as skilled a leader as John Smith had been, and soon the discipline of the colony disappeared. The Indians got tired of supplying the settlers with food, and relations with the Indians got worse. When any of the settlers left the fort in search of food, the Indians attacked and killed them.

The remaining settlers in Jamestown, leaderless and incapable of feeding themselves, spent another horrible winter, which later was named "The Starving Time." They traded valuable tools for food, burned houses to keep warm, and ate whatever they could find including their animals, mice, and rats, but still many of the settlers died.

The ship that brought men who were to be the leaders of the colony encountered a hurricane en route to the Virginia Colony and was wrecked on Bermuda Island. The survivors of the hurricane built two ships out of the wreckage and resumed their voyage to Jamestown. They landed in Jamestown on May 24, 1610, and found only ninety colonists who had survived the winter. They found no crops, no housing, and no tools. The settlers were ready to return to England and boarded the ships and abandoned the Jamestown settlement. They got about ten miles down the James river when they met another boat that brought the news that Lord De La Warr, the newly appointed governor of Virginia, was on his way with three ships of supplies and 150 new colonists. Those on the ship who were trying to make their way back to England were ordered to return to the settlement and await Lord De La Warr's arrival.

Lord De La Warr's arrival brought an additional three hundred settlers, and he began to bring order back to the colony. He created some rules by which the colonists were governed. These laws were created to govern all parts of the life of the colony. It was called the *Articles, Laws, and Orders*, and these laws were strictly enforced. Relations with the local Indian tribes also improved.[3]

Another new governor, Sir Thomas Dale, arrived in 1611, and under his leadership three new colonies were created. The first colony was called Hampton; the second one was called Charles City; and the third one was called Henrico. Jamestown was made the capital of these colonies.

The purpose for the founding of the Virginia Colony was to

make money for the London Company. The Jamestown settlement had problems because there were not any minerals or crops or anything to make the colony economically viable for its sponsors. The colonists tried a number of businesses, such as making silk, glassmaking, lumber, sassafras, and pitch and tar sales, but none of these were successful.

According to a legend, Pocahontas, the young daughter of the Powhatan Indian chief, saved the life of John Smith after the Powhatan Indians captured him. Indian women grew the food for the people and Indian men grew tobacco, but somehow Pocahontas knew about the growing of tobacco and helped the settlers by showing them how to cultivate it and cure it. The tobacco that the Indians grew was too harsh for English taste, but John Rolfe acquired the seeds for the tobacco grown in Trinidad and South America, which was more to the English's liking. Once this crop was established, the colony began to prosper. The first crop of tobacco was sold in London in 1614. During this time Pocahontas converted to Christianity and changed her name to Rebecca. She was married to John Rolfe in 1614 with her father's approval. For the next eight years the colony had peace with the Indians.

In 1616 John Rolfe and Rebecca sailed to England, where she was presented to the court of James I, who was then king of England. On the return voyage she died of smallpox. The ship docked at Gravesend, and Rebecca was buried in the nave of St. George's Church. Because her son, Thomas, was sickly, he was left to be reared in England. Rebecca was twenty-two years old when she died. In 1635 Thomas came to Virginia to reclaim his heritage, both Indian and English.

The use of tobacco became the rage in Europe. Unfortunately, the growing of tobacco depleted the soil of nutrients in four to seven years, and new land had to be acquired to continue growing the crop. To solve this problem, the farmers and plantation owners simply moved westward, claiming more land for the growing of tobacco. The western boundaries of the colonies were never officially established and were considered to extend indefinitely toward the west.

By this time the London Company changed its name to the Virginia Company. In 1619 the Virginia Company allowed colonists to own land themselves. If a colonist paid for his voyage to the Virginia Colony, a family would receive two hundred acres of land; indentured servants, once through with their indenture contract, could receive fifty acres of land.

The Virginia Company created the Virginia General Assembly. The royal governor would still rule the colony, but the assembly would write the laws. The legislative body would be composed of the Governor's Council and the House of Burgesses. The governor chose men appointed to the Governor's Council. Men were elected to the House of Burgesses by male landowners. The establishment of the House of Burgesses was the beginning of self-rule in the Virginia Colony.

Because of the success of the new crop, the colony needed additional labor. In 1619 a Dutch ship brought twenty slaves from Africa. The colonists eagerly purchased the slaves to help them with the farming of the tobacco crop. These first slaves were really indentured servants and were freed once they fulfilled their contract.[4]

The Virginia Company never made any money for its investors and was finally dissolved in 1620. Because the king felt the colony had been poorly managed, he, King James I, dissolved the Virginia Company and made the colony a Crown Colony in 1624. He also disbanded the House of Burgesses, but it continued to meet anyway.

James I died in 1625, and his successor, Charles I, recognized the House of Burgesses. Because the colonists had this experience in self-government, they felt they could and should challenge the English government when Parliament attempted to tax the colonists. This was the beginning of our Revolutionary War, or War of Independence from England, the subject of book two in this series.

The Jamestown settlement suffered several disastrous fires that twice burned the settlement. After the fourth burning of the State House, the site was abandoned, and the capital was moved to Williamsburg in 1699. Thanks to the Rockefeller Foundation, much of Colonial Williamsburg has been restored, and you can see what life was like in Williamsburg during the eighteenth century.

The Massachusetts Colony

The Pilgrims were the first settlers in what would later be known as the Massachusetts Colony. The Pilgrims founded the Plymouth Colony, which was later absorbed by the Massachusetts Bay Colony. These pilgrims came seeking freedom of religion, something they were unable to practice in England. Massachusetts became the second colony to be formed in the new world; it was formed in the year 1620.

There was a period of time in history called the Reformation, which began in the year 1517 with Martin Luther, who was a Catholic monk. Luther protested against the corruption of the Catholic Church. Until this time there was only one Christian church, the Catholic Church, and although there were many abuses of power by the church leaders, the church did not reform itself. The head of the Roman Catholic Church is called the pope, and at the time of Luther he was Pope Leo X. He lived in Rome, Italy. The Reformation (re-formation) of the church was led by Martin Luther, John Calvin, and others, who wrote about the abuses of power of the Catholic Church, but the pope and the church bishops ignored their writings and continued with their abuse of power.

Up until this time, the Bible was written in Latin, which was not a language that many people could read or understand. The priests of the church told the people what the Bible said. Martin Luther, who lived in Germany, translated the Bible into German so the people could read the Bible themselves and wouldn't have to rely upon the priests to tell them what the Bible said. When the church still did not reform itself, the people who agreed with Martin Luther broke from the Catholic Church and formed a new church, which is today called the Lutheran Church.

Around 1370 John Wycliffe, who lived in England, tried to reform the church in England. He translated the Bible into English. John Wycliffe also believed the people should be able to read the Bible for themselves. A period of persecution followed after the Bible was translated into English. Anybody who was found with an English Bible in his or her possession was arrested by the church and made to forfeit his or her copy of the Bible.

The Church of England, however, was formed when King Henry VIII wanted to divorce his wife and marry Anne Boleyn. Henry's wife, Catherine of Aragon, had only one living child, and the child was a girl named Mary. Henry desperately wanted to have a male child, because male children were the ones to have preference for succeeding the old king after he died. When Catherine was not able to give birth to a boy, Henry sought to divorce her and marry somebody who would give him a son and heir.

The pope didn't want to grant Henry's divorce because Catherine was from Spain, and Spain was a very powerful country at that time. The pope couldn't risk causing a problem with Spain. After several attempts at getting a divorce, Henry eventually dissolved the Catholic Church in England and made himself the head of the English church. Today the monarch in England is still head of the Church of England, also called the Anglican Church. The Anglican Church is called the Episcopal Church in our country. Henry as head of this new church made few changes—the service was in English, not Latin, but not much else was changed with the big exception that the king became head of the church in England in the place of the pope.

Henry VIII, as head of the church, granted himself the divorce from Catherine, thus enabling him to marry Anne Boleyn. Unfortunately for poor Anne, she too gave birth to a girl, who was named Elizabeth. Elizabeth was queen at the time of the attempted founding of the Roanoke Colony. Later Anne Boleyn gave birth to a male baby, but he was born dead. Henry was desperate to have a male heir, and Anne Boleyn became unpopular with Henry since she had also given birth to a female child. Anne was eventually beheaded, and Henry was free to marry again with the hopes that a new wife would produce a male heir.

There was a great upheaval in England after Henry dissolved the Catholic Church and formed the Church of England. People who, like the Pilgrims, didn't want to follow the teachings of the Church of England or the Catholic Church found themselves being persecuted. In England there were those who wished to "purify" the English Church, and they called themselves Puritans. There were others who wished to separate themselves from the Church of England and they were called Separatists. The people who sailed on the Mayflower were Puritans and Separatists, as well as Strangers, those who wanted to come to the new world but were "strangers" to the Puritans and Separatists. The people named Strangers didn't come to the new colony for religious reasons; they came to make money.

After the reign of Elizabeth I, James I of Scotland became king in the year 1603. In Scotland he was known as James VI. When he became king, he ordered all Englishmen to follow the teaching of the Church of England. For those who refused, life was harsh. They were put in jail and some even executed. In order to practice their religion, they had to worship in secret. Some of the Pilgrims (Puritans) and the Separatists fled to Holland where they were free to practice their brand of Christianity. After living in Holland for a period of time, they feared that their children were going to become Dutch and forget their English heritage. The Puritans living in Holland decided to leave Holland and seek a new life of religious freedom in the new world.

The Puritans and Separatists still living in England asked the king to allow them to form a new colony in the new world.

Remember, the Virginia Colony had already been formed, and the people in England knew about it. In 1606 King James I chartered two joint stock companies, the London Company, which sought settlers for the Colony of Virginia. The Plymouth Company, as part of the Virginia Company, was given the land north of the northern boundary of the Virginia Company to settle. The Plymouth Company financially had not been very successful. In 1620 the old Plymouth Company obtained a charter for Northern Virginia, which was later named New England. At this time the boundaries were not clearly defined. Northern Virginia was any of the lands north of the Virginia Colony.

James I was happy to have the Puritans leave England. The Pilgrims were very happy to sail to Northern Virginia to escape the persecutions they faced in England. The Pilgrims obtained a patent from the London Virginia Company, the same London Company that founded Jamestown in Virginia. They were to be indentured servants for seven years to the Virginia Company, after which time they would be free. The area the Mayflower intended to sail to was called Northern Virginia, and it was the area around the Hudson River that would become New York State and New Jersey, across the river from Manhattan Island.

When the Pilgrims and Separatists decided to leave Holland, they pooled their money and purchased a boat called the Speedwell. The Puritans, who were still living in England, rented a ship called the Mayflower. The settlers from Holland were going to meet up with those in England, and both ships and passengers were going to go together to Northern Virginia. On the trip from Holland to England, the Speedwell sprang several leaks. The Puritans had to stop in Plymouth, England, for repairs. After several attempts to repair the Speedwell, it was found to not be seaworthy and it was abandoned. Those traveling on the Speedwell had to transfer to the Mayflower to continue their journey.

On September 16, 1620, 102 Pilgrims, Separatists, and Strangers sailed for the new world on the Mayflower. During the trip to Northern Virginia, the Mayflower was blown off course and ended up north of the boundaries of the Virginia Colony. The land they spotted was near present-day Cape Cod in what would become the Massachusetts Colony. Although the captain of the Mayflower tried to sail south toward the Hudson River, the ship was not able to sail south because of the currents in the Atlantic Ocean. The passengers on the Mayflower decided to form their colony there. Because they didn't arrive in "Northern Virginia," they were released from the obligation as indentured servants to the London Virginia Company.

On November 21, 1620, before they left the ship to search for a place to locate their colony, they drew up what is called the Mayflower Compact, which included the rules under which they were going to govern themselves. It served as their official constitution for many years at the Plymouth Colony.

The landing spot, known today as Plymouth Rock, can still be seen in Plymouth Harbor. One hundred two days after leaving England, or so it was said, the Pilgrims went ashore, stepping on the rock to keep out of the freezing water. When they stepped on the land, they sank to their knees and thanked God for getting them safely to the new world. The official records kept by the Plymouth Colony make no mention of their landing on Plymouth Rock, but nevertheless, the story has been kept alive by the presence of a rock in Plymouth harbor that has been deemed to be the rock the Pilgrims stepped on when going ashore for the first time.

The Pilgrims decided the area of Cape Cod was not a good place to form their colony because the Indians were very hostile in this area.

They spent a month exploring the area before deciding on a location near Plymouth Harbor to found their settlement. They were seeking an area with a deep harbor, where ships bringing supplies from England could dock; they also needed streams of fresh water for drinking and for watering their crops. They finally chose the area known today as Plymouth and began to build their homes. They called their colony Plymouth. The location of the first colony has been partially reconstructed in Plymouth, Massachusetts, and it is possible to visit there and see inside replicas of the tiny homes the Puritans built to form their new colony. There is also a reproduction of an Indian home located near Plymouth Colony.

The first winter was spent on the Mayflower, and it was a difficult winter; much illness and the cold weather claimed the lives of nearly half of the colonists, as well as many of the crew on the Mayflower. During the day the settlers went ashore to build their houses, and they returned to the Mayflower at night. The following spring they were able to move into their newly built houses. Once the people moved into their homes, the Mayflower returned to England.

On March 16, 1621, they were visited by one of the Indians living in the area. His name was Somoset; he was of the Abnaki tribe. To their surprise he spoke a little English, which he had learned from some of the English fishermen who had explored the area before the Pilgrims arrived. He introduced the settlers to another Indian named Squanto who was from the Wampanoag tribe. Several years before the Pilgrims came, Englishmen had captured Squanto and taken him back to England. It was during his time in captivity that he had learned English. While in England, Squanto met a ship captain who was willing to take

Squanto back to his tribe; in return Squanto was to enable the ship captain to develop trading relations with the Indians. When Squanto arrived back in his home area, he found that his entire tribe had died of diseases brought by the English and other fishermen who frequented the coast of New England. It was fortunate for the Pilgrims that he was living with the Abnaki tribe, for without his help they might not have survived those first rugged winters.

Squanto stayed with the Pilgrims and taught them valuable skills that enabled them to survive in the New England climate. He showed them how to grow corn, squash, and other foods that could be grown in the Massachusetts climate. Squanto also taught them how to tap the sap from the maple trees, which is how the maple syrup you use on your pancakes and French toast is made. The settlers were also taught which plants were poisonous and which had healing powers.

After the first successful harvest and to give thanks to God for enabling the settlers to survive their first year in their new homes, the Pilgrims invited Squanto and his tribe to a feast. The Pilgrim Governor, William Bradford, proclaimed a day of thanksgiving, and Squanto joined the pilgrims together with ninety other Indians for the celebration. Today we too celebrate this feast, and we call it Thanksgiving Day.

In March 1629 a new king in England, Charles I, granted a royal charter that confirmed the land grants of 1628 of three miles south of the Charles River to three miles north of the Merrimac River and westward to the Pacific Ocean. John Winthrop arrived with a Charter called the Massachusetts Bay Charter. In the year 1630 several ships arrived, bringing a thousand families who settled around what is now Boston. This colony was called the Massachusetts Bay Colony. It wasn't long before these English colonies had settled as far west as what is now known as New

Hampshire. The area we know as the New England states literally became a New England.

During the 1630s, over twenty thousand English settlers arrived in Massachusetts. John Winthrop was the first governor of the Massachusetts Colony and Boston was the capital. The colonists in Massachusetts operated independently of England. It had a representative government, meaning those who were members of the Puritan Church could vote. Members of other religions were forbidden to participate in the government, and many were expelled from the colony when they didn't obey the Puritan rules.

The original Puritan settlers had a relationship with the surrounding Indian tribes. The settlers purchased land from the Indians, and the Indians traded goods with the settlers. For a while it appeared they could all live together without hostilities. The Indians eventually realized that the more land they sold to the settlers, the more settlers arrived, and the new settlers wanted even more land. The Indians were quickly losing their homeland.

Although some of the tribes were friendly to the colonists, others were not. King Philip, whose Indian name was Metacom, was the son of Massasoit, the Indian chief who helped the Pilgrims survive their first winter. King Philip led a rebellion of some of the Indian tribes against the English settlers. It is known as King Philip's War, and the war began in 1675 after some Wampanoag warriors killed some of the settlers' cattle. The cattle had often gotten out of their pens and eaten some of the Indians' corn. The settlers retaliated by killing an Indian and the war escalated.

Other tribes joined King Philip and set out to drive the English settlers from the colony. The Indians burned several English settlements and confiscated the provisions that had been set-aside for the colonists to eat during the long New England winters. The war finally ended with the death of King Philip in 1677; it was a very bloody war because so many settlers and Indians were killed during the conflict. The war was devastating to both the Indians and the English settlers. Without the Indians, the lucrative trade with England all but came to an end, which was equally as damaging to the colonists as it was for the Indians, who by this time were depending upon English trade. It took quite awhile for the trade to return to what it was before King Philip's War took place.

This difference in government of the Massachusetts Colony came from an oversight in the charter. The Virginia charter specifically said the colony was to be governed from England; the Massachusetts charter did not specify this, and therefore the colonists began to govern themselves without any interference from England. Later when the king of England tried to tax the colonists and force other restrictions on them, they revolted. This was the beginning of our Revolutionary War.

The area now known as the state of Maine was annexed to Massachusetts in 1652. With the end of King Philip's War, the area was left without friendly tribes of Indians to help keep the unfriendly tribes at bay. New England was subject to various Indian attacks, especially on the western border of the colony. The various independent Puritan colonies within Massachusetts had to ask for help from the English government; they were united under the royal charter in 1691. James II became the royal governor of New England, and the independence of these Puritan colonies came to an end.

The Maryland Colony

The Maryland Colony was the third colony to be founded and the year was 1634. Its founding was somewhat different that the first two colonies. Virginia Colony was founded by the London Company (a group of London merchants), and the Massachusetts Colony, was founded first by the Pilgrims and later other Puritan settlements were formed in the area that was called Massachusetts Bay Colony. The Maryland Colony, however, was founded as a land grant colony (by Charles I who was then king of England) and given to Sir George Calvert and his son, Lord Baltimore. Lord Baltimore named the colony Maryland in honor of Queen Henrietta Maria, who was the wife of King Charles I. George Calvert died before he could begin the settlement of his colony; the charter was transferred to his son, Cecillus Calvert. Cecillus became Lord Baltimore upon his father's death and carried out the plans of his father to form a colony. Strangely enough, he did all his governing from England and never once crossed the Atlantic Ocean to see the colony. In 1661 he sent his son, Charles Calvert, to be governor of the colony.

Lord Baltimore was a Roman Catholic and wanted to establish a colony where Catholics could worship freely. In England at the time, there was still much fighting between those who were loyal to the Roman Catholic Church and those who were loyal to the Church of England. The charter he received granted equality in religion and civil freedoms to the colonists.

In 1634, two hundred Roman Catholic settlers sailed up the Potomac River and purchased, from the Indians, a village on St. Mary's River. The Indians abandoned their cabins and the cornfields as soon as the harvest was completed and turned the area over to the settlers. The Indians taught the settlers how to grow and prepare maize (corn) and other vegetables grown by the Indians. In turn the settlers sold them metal axes and woolen cloth in exchange for the turkeys and venison the Indians hunted. At this time the Indians were still using axes made out of rock, and a metal ax was a large improvement upon the tools with which they had to work. The settlers and the Indians lived peacefully together.

The boundaries of the charter granted to Lord Baltimore included the land bounded on the north by the fortieth parallel, on the south by the southern boundary of the Potomac River, to the east by the Atlantic Ocean, and to the west by the meridian passing through the source of the Potomac River. Today this area would include portions of Pennsylvania, West Virginia, and all of Delaware, and this resulted in boundary disputes later.

As required by the charter, Lord Baltimore was required yearly to send to the king two Indian arrows as proof of his loyalty to the king, and if any gold and silver were mined in the colony, one-fifth was to be paid to the king. Lord Baltimore could not tax his colonists without their consent; he could, however, coin money, make war and peace, establish courts, and pardon criminals. The laws governing the colony were to be made by Lord Baltimore and the freemen who lived in the colony. In the beginning all freemen were to attend the assembly and make laws jointly, but this proved too unwieldy, and an assembly of delegates was finally chosen.

Maryland was the first colony that practiced religious tolerance. In 1649 Maryland passed the Toleration Act, which guaranteed religious freedom to all who inhabited the colony.

Charles II became king of England after the execution of Charles I. Because Charles II had no children, his brother James II became king after the death of his brother. In 1688 Lord Baltimore was about to lose his charter for the Maryland Colony when James II was driven into exile to France, where he remained for the rest of his life. In 1691 Maryland became a royal province and remained a royal colony until 1715 when the Calvert family regained the charter once again.

The Connecticut Colony

Connecticut was the fourth colony to be formed, but before it was an English colony there were Dutch settlers in what became the Connecticut Colony. The Dutch had built a trading post on the river, later named the Connecticut River, so they could trade with the Indians. In the year 1631, English settlers of Puritan religious background first settled the area of Connecticut that bordered Long Island Sound. This area was part of a large land grant by Charles I given to the Earl of Warwick under the title of Connecticut. The English also had a few settlers in what later became the towns of Windsor and Wethersfield; both of these towns were close to the border of the Massachusetts Colony.

It was around 1630 when some of the settlers in the Massachusetts Colony became unhappy with the strict rules of the Puritan Church. Thomas Hooker was a popular minister in the town of Newtown, now called Cambridge, but the land was not good farming land, and Hooker's congregation needed more land for their crops and for their cattle. The Massachusetts Bay Colony was not eager to have him leave, but he was also unhappy with the strict Puritan rules. In 1635 when his congregation couldn't get permission to move, a few families from his congregation moved into Connecticut anyway. Thomas Hooker was to follow them with the balance of his congregation the next year.

In 1636 he and the remaining members of his congregation walked the distance from Newtown in the Massachusetts Bay Colony to the Connecticut Valley. They walked the entire way, bringing their belongings (including their cattle) with them. They met up with those who had left the year before and established the colony at Hartford.

Thomas Hooker had some very different ideas about how to govern this new colony. He didn't restrict the voting to church members only; all adult male landowners were given the right to vote. In 1639 this colony adopted the first written constitution, called The Fundamental Orders, as its law. This constitution stated that a governor could not serve two successive terms and no religious test was to be administered for citizenship. It also created a general court and a governing body with legislative, judicial, and administrative sections. The very first idea of a democratic form of government was established, as this "constitution" gave the right to vote to all adult males who were landowners.

The Reverend John Davenport and Theophilus Eaton, who was a farmer and a Puritan leader, soon joined Thomas Hooker and established the colony of New Haven in 1638. These men were not as enlightened as was Thomas Hooker, and the colony at New Haven strictly enforced the Puritan religious beliefs including dress and forms of worship. Voting in the colony was restricted only to members of the church.

Other early towns that were settled were Windsor in 1633, Wethersfield in 1634, and Saybrook in 1635. In 1636 Windsor, Hartford, and Wethersfield united to form the Connecticut Colony. The Colony of New Haven remained outside of this union.

After the death of Thomas Hooker, John Winthrop Jr. became the governor of the Colony of Connecticut. In 1660 the colony of New Haven and the colony of Connecticut desired to establish the boundaries between the two colonies. The colony of Connecticut felt that the land claimed by the New Haven Colony was part of the land grant given by Charles I to the Earl of Warwick, which was awarded in 1631; New Haven was founded in 1638. In order to settle this argument, the colony of Connecticut decided to apply for a charter from Charles II like the one granted to the Massachusetts Bay Colony. Charles II granted the colony a charter to include the New Haven Colony, and with it came almost unlimited power for the colony to govern itself free from the rule of England. New Haven was not happy about being absorbed into the Connecticut Colony, but they were officially united in 1662.

As more and more settlers arrived, it was necessary for these settlers to purchase the land they occupied from the Quinnipiacs Indians and the Paugusset Indians. The Indians sold the land for English cloth, blankets, kettles, hatchets, hoes, knives, spoons, and mirrors. In turn the settlers promised to defend these friendly tribes from the hostile Indian tribes of Pequot and Mohawks.

In 1643 the Connecticut Colony, the New Haven Colony, the Massachusetts Bay Colony, and the Plymouth Colony had all been joined together and were known as the Confederation of New England.

In 1687 King James II wished to consolidate the charters of all the English colonies north of Pennsylvania, which would make them easier to govern. He called this confederation the Dominion of New England. In October of 1687, Sir Edmund Andros arrived to take away the Connecticut charter and establish himself as the governor of the area to be known as the Dominion of New England.

The colonists called an assembly during which Sir Edmund Andros demanded the return of the Connecticut charter. During the discussion all the candles were mysteriously extinguished; when they got the candles relit, the charter had disappeared. For years people believed Captain Wadsworth of Hartford had taken the charter and hidden it in the hollow of an old oak tree; the tree was called Charter Oak, but when the tree died in 1856, no charter was found, and the charter has never been found.

James II was deposed in 1688, and Connecticut joined with the other colonies in the Dominion of New England and ousted Andros as the royal governor thus ending the control by England over the Dominion of New England.

The Rhode Island Colony

Rhode Island was the fifth colony to be formed. The founding of Rhode Island came about because Roger Williams, who was a Puritan minister in the Massachusetts Colony, believed in religious freedom, and that could not be tolerated in the strictly Puritan Colony of Massachusetts Bay. The punishment for not following the Puritan belief precisely was expulsion from the Massachusetts Colony. Had Roger been caught, he would have been captured, arrested, and returned to England; the year was 1636.

After narrowly escaping arrest by the Puritan leaders, Roger Williams and five of his followers sought refuge with the Wampanoag Indians. This was the same Indian tribe that helped the Pilgrims survive their first winter in the Plymouth Colony. After spending the winter with the Indians, he traveled to the area he thought was outside the boundaries of the Plymouth Colony, but it wasn't. When Roger and his colonists learned this, they had to move again—this time to the area that is today known as Rhode Island. Once there he purchased land from the Indians and founded the town on Aquidneck Island, which he called Providence.

Other banished Puritans were Anne Hutchinson, William Coddington, and John Clarke. They too were forced to move from the Massachusetts Colony. They traveled to Rhode Island and founded the town also on Aquidneck Island, which they named Portsmouth. Later, William Coddington left Portsmouth and founded another town that was called Newport. The settlers in the towns on Aquidneck Island decided to rename the island Rhode Island, which later became the name for the entire colony.

Remember, the Puritans migrated from England because they didn't wish to be forced to follow the doctrines of the Church of England, and it seems strange that they ended up preventing anything but the strict observance of the Puritan religion in their colony of Massachusetts.

Rhode Island was a poorer colony than either the Massachusetts Bay Colony or the Plymouth Colony, as these colonies were formed by charters and had financial backing from investors in England.

This colony was formed to give religious freedom to all men, and as word spread back to the Massachusetts colonies, other settlers began to arrive and form other settlements in Rhode Island. This colony was more of a democracy, as all men, heads of households, were given the right to vote. As a means of governing themselves, they wrote an article of agreement:

Every male member of the town of Providence was asked to sign the article of agreement, which bound him to civil obedience, meaning obedience to the rules for running the colony, not religious obedience. In other words, each colonist could decide for himself which, if any, religion he was going to follow.

"We, whose names are hereunder written, being desirous to inhabit in the town of Providence, do promise to submit ourselves, in active or passive obedience, to all such orders or agreements as shall be made for public good by body in an orderly way, by the major consent of the inhabitants, masters of families, incorporated together into a township, and such others as they shall admit into the same, only in civil things."[5]

These new settlements feared being absorbed into either the

Massachusetts or Connecticut colonies, so in the summer of 1643, Rodger Williams sailed from New Amsterdam, now New York City, to England to obtain a royal charter. In 1644 he was granted a charter establishing Rhode Island as a separate colony. This charter was granted by Parliament in the name of the king and united the towns of Providence, Portsmouth, and Newport under the name of "the Incorporation of Providence Plantations in the Narragansett Bay in New England." Rhode Island became a haven for others experiencing persecution from the Puritans.

In the meantime, back in England, James I died and his son Charles I became king. James I had pushed England nearly to bankruptcy because of his excessive spending on artwork and his wars with the king of France. He had also married a Catholic, and the people were fearful he would attempt the restoration of the Catholic Church in England. Charles was out of money to fund his wars, and he was left with no choice but to call Parliament into session to ask for more money. Parliament refused to grant Charles I any funds. In 1642 Parliament stripped Charles of some of his remaining power. They placed the army and navy under the control of Parliament and removed the feudal means of extracting taxes and finally executed Charles in 1649. There followed a period of English civil wars. England was governed by Parliament without a king. This period in history was called The Commonwealth. Parliament proved as inept at governing as the king had been, and the monarchy was restored in 1660. Charles II became king in 1660 and ruled until 1688 when he died. After his death, his brother became king and ruled as James II.

When the monarchy was restored, the charter was considered invalid because it had been granted by Parliament. In 1663 Roger Williams went back to England to secure another charter from Charles II for Rhode Island and Providence Plantations. The new charter granted the same privileges to the settlers as the first charter. The charter included a land grant and provided for religious freedoms. Unfortunately, the legislature of the colony declared that Roman Catholics would not be included. In spite of this restriction, the settlers in Connecticut and Rhode Island enjoyed the greatest amount of freedom of the colonies.

The Delaware Colony

The colony of Delaware was the sixth colony to be formed. It holds a special place in history because it was the only colony to be a colony of two other countries before it became an English colony.

An Englishman, Henry Hudson, first discovered this area in the year 1609; however, the Dutch claimed jurisdiction over the territory because Henry Hudson, at this time, was in the service of the Dutch East India Company. Henry Hudson explored the Hudson River as far north as the town we now know as Albany, New York; he claimed this entire area for the Dutch and named it New Netherland. In 1631 Dutch traders established the first settlement in Delaware. It was located near the present town of Lewes. This settlement of only thirty people was found to be deserted later in 1631 when the Dutch ship captain returned and found all the settlers had been killed by the Indians.

A second settlement was made in 1638 when Swedish colonists established a colony near present-day Wilmington. These settlers built a fort on land they purchased from the Indians. They occupied the northern part of what we call the state of Delaware and named it New Sweden. Other Swedish settlements were located as far north as present-day Trenton, New Jersey, and Philadelphia, Pennsylvania. They claimed this area and named it New Sweden

The Dutch, not wishing to give up their claim to the area,

built a fort named Fort Casimir, which was located near the present-day town of New Castle in Delaware. It wasn't long before a Swedish war ship destroyed this fort. In retaliation Governor Stuyvesant (who was governor of New Amsterdam, called New York City today) sent other Dutch ships to the area and took back the area from Sweden.

The Dutch West India Company began to operate in New Netherland with the purpose of making money. They hoped to encourage settlers to come to New Netherland to begin a whaling and fishing community. From the Delaware River (this river separates the states of New Jersey and Pennsylvania) ships could sail into the Atlantic Ocean and bring goods back to the Netherlands (Holland). This industry was not successful.

New Sweden was supposed to also bring riches to Sweden in the form of the growing and selling of tobacco. The colony was successful until the Dutch regained control of the area and it returned to New Netherland's control.

A period of peace ensued until 1664 when the English defeated the Dutch in New Amsterdam and renamed the area New York. They also obtained the area of New Sweden and New Netherland and named the colony Delaware after the then-governor of the colony of Virginia, Lord De La Warr. Under the English the boundaries of the colony were disputed. At one point Lord Baltimore of the Maryland Colony claimed the area as part of Maryland. In 1678 the northern boundary was finally settled, and it was settled in a circular configuration, extending into the colony of Pennsylvania but stopping short of including Philadelphia.

In 1682 William Penn, of the Pennsylvania Colony, purchased the three lower colonies from Delaware and made them part of Pennsylvania. Lord Baltimore disputed the purchase, and he and William Penn went to England to ask the king to decide who owned the territories in question. In November 1685 it was decided that the area in question was to be equally divided between William Penn and the Delaware Colony.

William Penn created three counties in Pennsylvania and named them Philadelphia, Chester, and Bucks. The three lower counties given to Delaware were named New Castle, Kent, and Sussex. These lower counties were then divided into *hundreds*, which was the English way of dividing land. This remains the name in Delaware for county divisions. Delaware is the only state that uses the term hundreds for county divisions.

The Delaware Colony began to grow tobacco as well as wheat and cotton. When the growing of tobacco became profitable, slaves were imported to work on the farms. After the Revolutionary War the slave trade in Delaware was banned. Farmers who owned slaves at the end of the Revolution were allowed to keep their slaves, but no new slaves could be brought into Delaware.

After the Revolutionary War was won and the Constitution written, Delaware was the first state to ratify the new Constitution.

The New Hampshire Colony

The New Hampshire Colony was the seventh colony to be established. King James I wished to promote settlement in what was called New England, and in 1622 the council he formed for this purpose granted six thousand acres to David Thomson. He and twenty men who traveled with him built one of the first settlements in New Hampshire; it was named Pannaway Plantations. This settlement also included a fort where they traded with the Indians.

Also in the year 1620, James I of England granted a charger to the Council of New England to encourage the settlement of the northeast. The man who was head of this council was Sir Ferdinando Gorges. A few years later, Sir Gorges added John Mason as an investor in the project. John Mason named the area New Hampshire because he was from a county in England called Hampshire. They also acquired the land that later became the state of Maine. At this time it was called the Province of Maine. They were given the land between the Merrimack and Sagadock Rivers.

The joint stock company that administered the colony was dissolved after a few years because it was not making any money. The land was divided in the year 1629. Sir Ferdinando Gorges was given the land east of the middle of the Pascatagua River that was named Maine, and Mason kept the land between the

Piscatagua and the Merrimac rivers and kept the name New Hampshire.

Unlike the settlers in Massachusetts, the settlers in New Hampshire came to make money. They hoped to develop trade with Indians and sell furs, timber, and fish to England.

In 1635 John Mason died. His heirs in England didn't take care of his land grant, and others began to settle on his land. The colony in Massachusetts also began to claim land in the New Hampshire Colony. In 1638 Robert T. Mason tried to reclaim his grandfather's land, which caused a dispute between Massachusetts and New Hampshire. The result was that the land became a royal province on January 1, 1680. The problem still wasn't settled, and the same royal governor ruled the Massachusetts and New Hampshire Colonies until the year 1741. New Hampshire petitioned the king for a settlement of the boundaries between the two colonies. New Hampshire won and regained some territory and its own royal governor.

The two oldest permanent settlements in New Hampshire are Dover and Portsmouth. Dover was a fishing and trading settlement, and Portsmouth became a center for shipbuilding.

In 1638 the Reverend John Wheelwright (who was expelled from the Massachusetts Bay Colony) purchased land from the Indians and formed the town of Exeter. Several other families who wanted to escape from the harsh Puritan rules in the Massachusetts Bay Colony joined him in his new town of Exeter.

Wheelwright and his followers wrote a document for the government of his new colony. It established procedures for the election of officials, taxation, a ban on selling liquor to the Indians, and allowed a trial by jury for those who broke the laws. A few years later, the settlers petitioned the Massachusetts Bay Colony to absorb Exeter into the colony of Massachusetts Bay. Wheelwright and his family moved to the village of Wells in the province of Maine. This was not a Puritan community, and after some time Wheelwright wrote to the General Court in the Massachusetts Bay Colony asking to be re-admitted to the colony. The ban against Wheelwright was lifted, but he remained in Wells while waiting for a church position to open for him.

In 1648 the town of Hampton (now located in New Hampshire) asked him to be their minister. He returned to England for a brief period of time, but King Charles II was persecuting Puritans, and Wheelwright returned to New Hampshire. He was minister in Salisbury, New Hampshire, at the time of his death.

The town of Londonderry was settled in 1719 by some Scotch-Irish immigrants who began the growing of flax and manufactured linen cloth, which became very popular in New England and was exported to England.

The industry in New Hampshire followed the coastline (shipping and fishing businesses were on the coast and along the rivers); textile and lumber mills also sprang up along waterways. The farming areas were inland.

Boundary disputes between the colonies of New York Colony and Massachusetts Bay Colony were finally settled in 1741.

The North Carolina Colony

North Carolina was the eighth colony to be formed, followed by its twin sister, South Carolina. The people from Virginia formed North Carolina in 1653. The first settlement was made on the banks of the Chowan and Roanoke rivers, which became known as Albemarle.

Charles II, king of England, granted a charter to eight lords proprietor for the land south of Virginia. The boundaries on the map were settled at twenty-nine degrees north latitude to thirty-six degrees, thirty minutes (which was the southern boundary of the Virginia colony), extending from the Atlantic Ocean to the Pacific Ocean. These early explorers had no idea how vast a country they were attempting to settle.

One of the lords proprietor (Lord Albemarle) founded a county named Albemarle county and divided it into four precincts, which selected representatives for an assembly; the balance of the government for the colony consisted of an appointed court, council, and governor. The proprietors were poor administrators, and the government was unstable. When the colony of Carolina was divided into two separate colonies, North and South Carolina, Albemarle became known as North Carolina and Charleston became South Carolina.

The Charleston settlement (Charles Town) grew rapidly, as did Albemarle, but both settlements suffered from poor administration, including internal conflicts from settlers of differing nationalities: the French Huguenots (French Protestants) who settled in Bath, near Pamlico Sound; the Germans from the Rhine who founded a town named New Berne near the junction of the Trent and Neuse rivers; the English settlers, many of them Quakers (more about the Quakers when we get to the founding of Pennsylvania); and some Scotch-Irish, who settled the town of Ulster.

Because the settlements continued to experience conflict and bad governing, George II bought the shares of Carolina from seven of the lords proprietor in 1729, and it became a royal colony. The population grew from thirty thousand settlers in 1729 to two hundred sixty-five thousand in 1776.

In the hopes of attracting settlers to North Carolina, several mistakes were made. One of the enticements exempted the new settlers from paying taxes for a year. Those settlers who were in debt in other colonies had their debts excused when they moved to Carolina. Also a settler could not be sued in Carolina for anything that occurred in another colony. Unfortunately, these actions got settlers to the area, but many were individuals, criminals, and scoundrels. These differing settlers came into conflict with one another over matters of religion too. The royal governor attempted to establish the Church of England as the religion of the colony, and that caused another round of conflicts.

For most of the period of the Royal Colony, the settlements were formed on the coast of Carolina. As more and more Germans and Scotch-Irish settlers arrived (including those who were running away from debts in other colonies), the settlers began to move farther inland to form new settlements. As the settlements expanded farther west, they came in conflict with the Indians of the area. In 1711 a terrible massacre of the settlers by the Indians occurred, and many of the German settlers in New Berne were killed. The settlers in the North Carolina Colony retaliated and received aid from the South Carolina Colony. This time many Indians were killed. The Tuscaroras Indians, who were originally from the New York area, returned home and, together with the Iroquois and other tribes, formed the Indian Confederation known as the Six Nations. We will discuss more of the Six Nations when we get to the Indian Wars.

The settlers in the backcountry, those who moved closer to the Allegheny Mountains, lived an entirely different type of life than those who settled on the coast. The coastal settlers were slaveholders and grew tobacco in the area near the Virginia border, rice on the Cape Fear River, and grain and cattle. Between the backcountry and the coastal settlements was a large forest of pine trees. The trees provided tar, turpentine, and lumber for export. Farmers and woodsmen settled the backcountry. They lived apart in towns and small settlements that were scattered throughout the backcountry; no large cities grew up in the backcountry—only small, scattered settlements.

The South Carolina Colony

As you know, North Carolina and South Carolina were created at one time as the colony of Carolina; it wasn't until 1729 that the two colonies were divided and became two separate colonies. North Carolina became the eighth colony, and South Carolina became the ninth colony to be formed.

Although there were several attempts to found a colony on the Carolina coast, none of them succeeded until the eight nobles acquired a royal charter from King Charles II and founded the two towns that later became North Carolina (Albemarle) and South Carolina (Charleston).

From the beginning of the settlement in South Carolina, the people governed themselves with a representative assembly, rather than being ruled by the agents of the king in England. There was a clause in the charter given by the king, which gave the right of making laws to the freemen who lived in the colony. The governors of the colony ruled the colony together with the representative assembly. Many of the governors were poor administrators and stole from the colonists. In 1687 the governors attempted to introduce some strict rules for governing, and the colonists resisted and removed those governors who did nothing more than plunder the colony for their own enrichment. With the successful removal of the ineffective governors, a period of peace and prosperity resulted.

When Louis XIV of France revoked the Edict of Nantes,

which had granted the French Protestants the right to worship their own way, a period of repression and forced Catholicism began. Louis XIV not only forced the Huguenots to return to Catholicism but also forbid them to leave France. Many Huguenots died trying to escape, but nearly five hundred thousand were able to leave France, and some of those who escaped settled in South Carolina.

When Sir Nathaniel Johnson became governor in 1703, trouble began again for the settlers because he passed a law excluding all those who didn't wish to worship in the manner of the Church of England. The assembly voted to repeal the law, but Sir Johnson refused to sign the bill. The colonists appealed to the House of Lords in England and won; the proprietors, who were threatened with the loss of their charter, yielded, and the dissenters regained control of the government.

A little background information on world history is needed here. The years 1400–1500 were the years of the explorers. Spain was a powerful country at that time and was eager for the gold the explorers found in Central and South America. In the year 1493 both Spain and Portugal claimed the same lands in South and Central America. They appealed to Pope Alexander VI, and he drew a line dividing the world not held by a Christian ruler. He gave all the land west of the line of demarcation to Spain, and to Portugal the land east of it. In 1494 Portugal protested the division, and the pope moved the line 930 miles west, which gave the country now known as Brazil to Portugal. This is why today Brazil speaks Portuguese, not Spanish.

Because of this line of demarcation, Spain owned nearly all of Central and South America, including what is now Florida, Texas, New Mexico, Arizona, and much of California. Spain was not interested in colonizing the area like the English were; the Spanish wanted the gold found in the areas of South and Central America and were ruthless in acquiring the gold. Spanish priests also went to the new world to convert the Indians. Because of the close proximity of the Spanish in Florida, there were always skirmishes between the English and the Spanish. The Spanish in St. Augustine (Florida) caused the Indian War of 1715. After the defeat of the Spanish Armada (an armada is a large fleet of warships), a peace treaty was signed ending the war between England and Spain. This treaty was called the Treaty of Utrecht. The Spanish were mad about losing the war with England and were determined to destroy all the English settlements in the Carolinas. The Spanish hoped to get the Indians to kill the English settlers because some of the Indians were indebted to the English traders and didn't wish to pay their debts; the Indians were also angry because some of the white men had captured and sold some of the Indians into slavery. Provoked by the Spanish, the Indians began a war, and although many settlers were killed the Indians were finally subdued and driven into Florida, leaving the Carolinas in peace.

The war only lasted ten months but was quite expensive for the colonists, and they asked the lords proprietor, who were receiving a large income from the colony, to help pay the expenses of the war. The proprietors refused to help and refused to permit the assembly to raise money by creating import duties or by selling vacated Indian lands. The people rebelled and asked the king to make South Carolina a Royal Colony. The king agreed and the charter was withdrawn, basically because the proprietors were unable to govern the colony properly. In 1719 South Carolina became a Royal Colony.

As a Royal Colony, South Carolina prospered and grew rapidly. The growing of rice became a crop for export, along with indigo, a plant that produced a dark blue fluid used as a dye. The other products for export were furs, cattle, forest products, and later, cotton. Because the growing of rice was so difficult, slaves were imported to do the backbreaking work. South Carolina became the biggest slaveholding colony.

At the end of the Indian war, another large immigration of peoples came. Among them were five hundred Irish settlers to occupy the land vacated by the Indians. Other immigrants to the area came from Virginia, Pennsylvania, and North Carolina. South Carolina had a major seaport (Charleston), which gave it access for trading, and as a result it encouraged a steady inflow of settlers.

The New Jersey Colony

New Jersey was the tenth English Colony to be formed. Before it was a British Colony, the Dutch claimed most of the land, and it was part of what they called New Netherland. For a short time part of western New Jersey, around Trenton, was also claimed by Sweden. The Dutch established a trading post on Manhattan Island (New York City now) and named the island New Amsterdam. In 1628 Peter Minuit was appointed the director of the Dutch colonies, and he purchased the island of New Amsterdam from the Indians.

John Cabot, an English explorer, explored the east coast of America, and in the year 1497 he claimed the entire east coast for England. By 1664 New Netherland was the only non-English settlement on the entire east coast. The English didn't like having part of the area (Delaware, New Jersey, New York, and parts of New England) owned by another country. The Dutch's fur trading with the Indians was cutting into the profits for the English, and the English king, Charles II, decided to take New Netherland from Dutch control.

In the fall of 1664, Charles sent four warships to New Amsterdam and told the Dutch governor (Peter Stuyvesant) to surrender the land to England. Peter Stuyvesant gave up the land without a fight. The English renamed New Amsterdam New York City. The Dutch settlers were allowed to stay in their colonies as long as they swore allegiance to the English king.

The English established the New Jersey Colony in the same year. New Jersey became the land between the Hudson River on the east and the Delaware River on the west. King Charles II gave the colony to his brother, James the Duke of York. In turn James gave this area to two of his friends, Lord Berkeley and Sir Philip Carteret, who were the proprietors (owners) of the land. Philip Carteret became the governor and together with some others founded a settlement and named it Elizabethtown.

There were not many settlers in New Jersey when it became an English colony, and for it to be a successful colony, it was necessary to attract more settlers. Settlers from other colonies were encouraged to relocate to New Jersey. The proprietors of New Jersey also offered settlers in New Jersey freedom of religion.

Some of the previously mentioned original settlers of New Haven Colony were unhappy when New Haven became part of the Connecticut Colony and decided to move to New Jersey. These Puritans founded the town of Newark. They bought the land directly from the Hackensack Indians. The Indians sold the land for some gunpowder, axes, coats, swords, kettles, blankets, hoes, knives, ten pairs of breeches, and three trooper coats. The settlers arrived in May 1666, and in 1676 they purchased additional land roughly equivalent to what is now Essex County. This village was first named Milford, because that was the name of the town in Connecticut from which most of them came. It was later renamed Newark in honor of their first minister who was ordained at Newark-on-Trent in England.

The colony was named New Jersey because Sir Philip Carteret had been born on the island of Jersey, which is a large island located off the coast of England.

The type of government for the colony established by Sir Philip Carteret was to be a three-part government, with Carteret as governor, a council, and an assembly of twelve men to be chosen by the people. He granted religious liberty to the

Englishmen who came to the new colony. One important thing to note here was there were to be no taxes assessed without the consent of the assembly. This will be important when we get to the Revolution and the resulting Declaration of Independence from England. For the first five years of the colony, land free of rent was given to anyone having a good musket and six months' provisions who migrated to New Jersey with the governor. The settlers who came later were charged a halfpenny-an-acre rent for the land. The first rent payments were due in 1670, and most of the settlers refused to pay the rent, telling the governor they had purchased the land from the Indians, who they said were the rightful owners. The people rose up against the governor, but they did not succeed. Lord Berkeley was upset by the problems between Carteret and his colonists, and he sold his portion of the colony to two Quakers, John Fenwick and Edward Byllynge. Edward Byllynge became bankrupt and sold his portion to trustees, including William Penn, who we will meet again in the formation of the Pennsylvania Colony.

The colony was divided in 1676 into two sections—East Jersey, which was owned by Carteret, and West Jersey, which was owned by the Quakers. Two separate governments were set up, and the first town in West Jersey was founded by 230 people and named Burlington; several hundred more settlers poured into this area. A Quaker government was established giving all power to the people, and no crimes were considered severe enough to result in the death penalty. Most of the Quaker settlements were along the Delaware River.

The Puritans who came from New England settled in East Jersey and established a form of government more severe than that created for West Jersey. East Jersey listed thirteen crimes for which a person could be put to death. In 1680 George Carteret died, and East Jersey was sold to twelve different men, one of whom was William Penn. Each of the twelve men in turn sold half of his interest to another man, and East Jersey then had twenty-four proprietors. The twenty-four men chose Robert Barclay as governor for life, and the colony was governed by Quaker rules until James II became king of England and took back the charter for both East and West Jersey.

James II united the colony with New York and the New England colonies. James II also appointed Sir Edmond Andros as the new governor. He was later deposed, and the heirs of Carteret and the Quakers again laid claim to the territory. Nothing was decided, and much confusion resulted when it was decided to give the entire colony back to the Crown; in 1702 it became the property of Queen Anne who was then the ruling English monarch. She gave the territory to the governor of New York. After thirty-six years of this arrangement, the two colonies were finally separated in 1738.

By 1746 New Jersey had two universities. The first one was called the College of New Jersey; later this college was renamed Princeton University. In 1752 Queen's College was formed to train ministers. Later this college was renamed Rutgers University, which is now the State University of New Jersey.

New Amsterdam—Manhattan Island (New York City)

New Netherland—the New York Colony

The New York Colony was the eleventh colony to be settled, but it started out first as a Dutch colony.

In 1609 an Englishman named Henry Hudson who was working for the Dutch East Indian Company explored the area along the coast of New Jersey and sailed up a river as far north as what we call Albany, New York. This river is now called the Hudson River after Henry Hudson. This river separates New Jersey from Manhattan Island. He and some Belgian settlers started a colony that they named New Netherland. The colony on the Island of Manhattan was called New Amsterdam and was settled in the year 1624.

The settlers purchased Manhattan and Long Island from the Indians for what today would be $24.99 in beads and other goods. The colony of New Netherland grew and eventually included what are today the states of New Jersey, Delaware, and the area that was known as New Sweden, which before the Dutch claimed it was part of Delaware, Maryland, western New Jersey, and Pennsylvania, up to what became Philadelphia.

The colonies of New Sweden and New Netherland did not have as many settlers as the English colonies. In order to attract more settlers to the Dutch colony, the government in Holland issued a charter of "Privileges and Exemptions" in 1629 that established the patroon system. Any member of the West India Company who would bring fifty settlers older than fifteen years of age would be granted an estate of sixteen miles frontage on one side of a river or bay and as far inland as the occupiers' could farm.

The valley of the Hudson River was filled with these little estates. The patroon was bound to provide a farm, fully stocked for each tenant, together with a schoolmaster and a minister of the Dutch Reformed Church; religious freedom in the Dutch colony did not exist. The tenants of the patroon were really nothing more than servants for ten years. The tenants were forced to sell their produce to the patroon and have their corn ground in the mill provided by the patroon; in addition they had to pay some rent during the ten years of service. Some of the family names of these early patroons are familiar names in the New York area today: Van Rensselaers, Schuylers, and Livingston. In order to get even more settlers to settle in New Netherland, the land was later opened to anybody from the British colonies of New England, Maryland, and Virginia who wanted to settle in New Netherland.

Peter Stuyvesant was one of several governors who strictly ruled the Dutch colony and allowed the colonists no freedom to govern themselves. English colonies surrounded the Dutch colonies, and the Dutch settlers knew that the English settlers were granted a say in their own colonial government and were not happy that the Dutch governors would not grant them the same freedoms. English settlements were on the north shore of Long Island, which was across Long Island Sound from the Connecticut Colony

For a long time Spain ruled the oceans, but with the defeat of the Spanish Armada during the reign of Elizabeth I of England, Spain was no longer the ruler of the seas. With Spain out of the picture, a rivalry between the Dutch and the English navies developed. Many of the goods made in the colonies and crops grown in the colonies, including tobacco, were shipped to England in Dutch ships.

England passed a Navigation Law in 1651 that required that all goods exported from the colonies would have to pay custom duties. Custom duties were taxes on imported goods that the receiving country had to pay. The Dutch ignored the law and continued to ship goods from the colonies without paying the custom duties. This meant a loss of income to the English government. With the Dutch colony sandwiched between the English colonies, the English government felt threatened and decided to send a small fleet of ships, with about five hundred English sailors, to capture the colony of New Netherland and make it an English colony. The Dutch settlers were not happy with Peter Stuyvesant and the previous Dutch governors, and when the English claimed the colony in 1664, the Dutch settlers gave up without a fight. They hoped to have more freedom under English rule than they had as a Dutch colony. The Dutch and Swedish settlers were required to pledge their loyalty to the British king, which they were happy to do.

When King Charles II of England became king, he gave the colonies of New Netherland and New Sweden to his brother who had the title of the Duke of York, and the colony was renamed New York in his honor.

Unfortunately for these colonists, the Duke of York proved

to be as unjust a governor as the Dutch governors had been. Remember that the colonies were established first and foremost to bring riches to the holders of the charters and the crown when they became Royal Colonies. England believed its colonies were extensions of the mother country and therefore were subject to the same taxes. The colonists were taxed to help pay for the war to defeat the Spanish and the war with the Dutch. As the taxes grew, so did the cries for freedom to govern themselves independent of English rule. The colonists were not represented in the English Parliament (similar to our House and Senate) and therefore did not have any say in the taxes that were imposed upon the colonies. The cry of "No Taxation without Representation" was the cry among the settlers. This would later become the battle cry for the beginning of the Revolution.

The oppression of the settlers in New York continued until William Penn (the founder of the Pennsylvania Colony) persuaded the Duke of York (in 1683) to allow an assembly of representatives to be elected. When they met they passed a law called the Charter of Liberties and Privileges, which was approved and would have given each free man the right to vote for people to represent him in the government of the colony. In addition, one of the liberties the colonists were given was the right of a trial by a jury and freedom of religion. The Charter of Liberties also provided that no colonist was to be taxed without the approval of the assembly; and religious freedom was also established. The government of the colony was to be a three-branch government, consisting of the governor, council, and the general assembly. The governor of New York and the duke both approved the charter, but it was unsigned when Charles II died.

After Charles II died, his brother, the Duke of York, became the new king; he ruled as James II of England. It was at this point that the colony became a Royal Colony. James refused to sign the Charter of Liberties and Privileges and abolished the

New York assembly. He in turn sent Sir Edmond Andros to govern the colonies of New York, New England and New Jersey.

The New York Colony continued to grow with ever-increasing numbers of Huguenots, Scots, Irish, and German settlers coming to the colony. By 1750 there were around eighty thousand settlers in this colony. Because of its location, New York soon became a major shipping center for the colonies.

The Pennsylvania Colony

The Pennsylvania Colony was the twelfth colony to be founded. William Penn's father was Admiral Penn, and at his death King Charles II owed him sixteen thousand pounds. I don't know how much that would be in American dollars today, but needless to say it was a sizeable amount of money at the time. William Penn went to the king and instead of asking for payment of the debt owed to his father, Penn asked for some land in the new world where he could establish a colony where his fellow Quakers could worship God in the Quaker manner. He asked for some territory west of the Delaware River, which separates Pennsylvania and New Jersey now, and from the northern boundary of Maryland north to as far as plantable land could be found. What he was granted was forty thousand square miles. Pennsylvania means Penn's Woods as the terrain was heavily forested.

At the time of Penn's birth, the Church of England was the only religion allowed to be practiced in England. When William Penn was a teenager, his family moved to Ireland. It was there that William became acquainted with Thomas Lowe and the religion of the Quakers.

The Quakers do not have any clergymen and do not believe that it was necessary to have a minister/priest for them to communicate with God. The Quakers believed that their word was law and therefore would never swear an oath. They were peace loving and refused to fight in any wars or to pay taxes to support any wars.

William Penn became a member of the Quaker religion, and he too suffered from the religious intolerance in England. He was arrested for his beliefs and spent some time in the Tower of London (used as a jail for political prisoners), but he still refused to give up his beliefs in the Quaker religion. When he realized he was not able to change the religious attitude in England, he decided he wanted to establish a colony in the new world that truly would become a land of religious tolerance for his fellow Quakers.

William Penn was granted a charter to govern his territory. He owed the king, as a token of his allegiance to the crown, two beaver skins and also one-fifth of the gold and silver that might be mined in Pennsylvania each year. As proprietor of this new colony, William Penn was given the power to establish courts, appoint judges, train soldiers, which is interesting since he was a Quaker and wouldn't fight in a war anyway, to wage wars, and to make laws to govern his colony. The king reserved the right to veto any laws he didn't like, and also, and this is important for the beginning of the Revolutionary War, the ability to tax the colony was left with the English Parliament. Parliament is composed of the House of Lords and the House of Commons. Members of the House of Commons were elected, but the House of Lords, at that time, was comprised of inherited seats.

Because the land grant from the king was part of what had been New Sweden and New Netherland, there were people already settled in the new colony. The representative of William Penn arrived to assure those settlers they would be free to continue to worship God in the manner they wished. He also met with representatives of the local Indian tribes to assure them that he wished to live in harmony with them. William Penn also made a treaty with the Indians to assure them that he and his colonists wished to live in peace and friendship with them. Although this treaty was not a written one (because that would not be allowed by the Quaker religion), William Penn had given his word and that was law. The colonists lived peacefully with the Indians.

William Penn built a city that was to be the capital of the colony. He called this city Philadelphia, which is a Greek word that means "brotherly love." The construction for the capital began in 1681, and he designed it to be open and roomy in order to not re-create the crowded conditions of London streets. It was here that the framers of the Constitution met in the summer of 1775 to write the Declaration of Independence and later the Constitution of the United States.

The government of this colony was very liberal in comparison with some of the other colonies. When William Penn arrived in the New World and reached the settlement of Chester, he called a provisional legislature and gave land to settlers and framed laws to govern the colony. In 1683 the new government had two branches, a council that originated the laws and an assembly that approved the laws but couldn't propose laws; later this was changed, and both branches could propose laws. William Penn was the first governor. All freemen were citizens and could vote for people to be members of the council and the assembly. The colony passed laws to educate children, give employment to criminals, and allow religious toleration.

Because of its liberal government and Penn's views of religious freedom, this colony soon surpassed New York in population, even though New York had been founded earlier.

Because of a border dispute between Lord Baltimore (Maryland Colony) and William Penn (Pennsylvania Colony), Penn and Baltimore went back to England to have the dispute settled. Penn was accused of supporting the dethroned king and was deprived of the colony. The colony was then given to Governor Fletcher of New York to govern. Penn's rights to the colony were restored in 1692, and he went back to Pennsylvania. In his absence the colonists of Delaware were demanding a separate government, and William Penn granted it to them. The colonists were also beginning to demand greater freedoms, and the new government basically transferred all power for governing themselves to the people. They still had to give allegiance to the English crown; the governor still had veto power over any laws submitted. This remained the constitution of Pennsylvania until after the Revolutionary War.

In order to get new settlers, William Penn advertised for settlers to come to his colony. He printed pamphlets and sent them to various countries in Europe and England. A man in Germany named Francis Pastorius read Penn's pamphlet and purchased fifteen thousand acres of land from William Penn with the hope of creating a German settlement in Pennsylvania. Those first German families who came were given three acres of land to farm, and he named his new town Germantown. Germantown is still in existence today. These German settlers came with established skills as papermakers, blacksmiths, potters, and coopers (who made barrels for the storage of food etc.), which helped strengthen the economy of the colony.

Because William Penn offered lands to new settlers cheaply (ten dollars per hundred acres), total religious freedom, and a nearly democratic government, Pennsylvania became an attractive place for people suffering religious persecution in other countries.

The once powerful Catholic Church was threatened when the Reformation movement took hold in Europe and England. In fact there was much upheaval in Europe during the 1500s and 1600s because of the Reformation. As noted, the Reformation was a religious movement begun to correct the abuses of the Catholic Church. Because people who wanted to worship God in a different way than the Catholic Church were persecuted, large numbers of people from Europe and England, as well as people from other colonies who wanted the freedoms Pennsylvania offered, began to immigrate to the Pennsylvania Colony.

By 1750 Philadelphia was the largest city in the British colonies. Philadelphia was a port city even though it didn't front on the Atlantic Ocean. It was located on the Delaware River, which was a deep river where ships coming from other countries could dock and unload their cargos and from which goods produced in the colony could be shipped back to England. It was also a port of entry for people who wanted to immigrate to the colony.

One of the very interesting groups that settled in Pennsylvania is a group called the Amish. They were a religious group from Switzerland and southern Germany who wanted a more secluded lifestyle; they established their community in Lancaster, Pennsylvania. There are still Amish farms in Lancaster today. The Amish sill live in the same way they did when they first settled Lancaster County. They don't drive cars and get around by horse and buggy. They don't use electricity and therefore do not have televisions or DVD players. They and their children dress in the manner of people from the seventeenth century. Although they learn English in school, they prefer to speak to one another in a German dialect. Most of the Amish live on farms and produce their own food.

Other small religious groups to settle in Pennsylvania were the Moravians, from Germany, who established the town of Bethlehem, Pennsylvania. There were other minority groups such as the Mennonites, whose lifestyle is similar to the Amish, who also found refuge in Pennsylvania.

The Georgia Colony

The Georgia colony was the last colony of the original thirteen colonies to become an English colony; it was settled in 1733. James Oglethorpe, who was a member of the British Parliament, was concerned about the condition of the debtors' prisons in England and the people who were imprisoned there because they couldn't pay their debts. At this time in English history, if someone could not pay off his debts, the person he owed money to could have the debtor put in prison until he could pay or someone paid his debts for him. This always seemed a silly way to punish someone, as a debtor couldn't work while in prison and therefore the debt might never be repaid; nevertheless, that was the law in England at this time.

Before Georgia was an English colony, Spain attempted to join it to Spanish Florida. Spanish missionaries built Catholic missions in the area. The purpose of these missions was to convert the Indians to Catholicism, to make slaves (sell the Indians into slavery to work on Spanish plantations in the Caribbean), and to force the Indians to mine for gold. After several Indian revolts, the Spanish missionaries were run out of the area we know as Georgia. English laid claim to the area south of the colony of South Carolina and North of Spanish Florida, and settlers from South Carolina and other colonies began to move into the area.

The vacuum caused by the vacating Spanish gave rise to the land being overrun by pirates. Georgia was swampy, full of little islands and marshlands. Georgia became the perfect place for pirates such as Blackbeard to hide.

There were several notorious pirates during the time of the thirteen colonies. Henry Morgan was one; Blackbeard was another; Captain Kidd and Bonny and Read were other famous pirates. Bonny was an infamous woman pirate. Because Spain was shipping large amounts of gold and silver from the areas we know as Mexico, Central, and South America, pirates patrolled the Atlantic Ocean to capture these Spanish ships and keep the treasures for themselves.

Blackbeard was known as "the Terror" and also Blackbeard because of his long black hair and beard. He must have been quite a frightening spectacle because as he boarded captured ships, he had long lighted matches—those used to light the cannons on his ship—stuck in his hair and beard. He was so feared that when his ship was sighted, ship captains often gave up without a fight. Pirates flew flags using some form of skull and crossbones, but Blackbeard's flag was a skeleton holding a spear dripping with blood.

The English didn't care if Blackbeard attacked Spanish ships but drew the line when he attacked English vessels. Unfortunately for Blackbeard, he also attacked merchant ships bringing goods into the colonies. The merchants in the Carolina colonies, whose merchandise was being stolen by Blackbeard, asked their governor to do something. The governor was a partner of Blackbeard's, so he ignored the request of his merchant settlers. Finally, in desperation, the merchants sent a group of merchants to the governor of Virginia and asked for his help in getting rid of Blackbeard. The governor ordered two naval ships to search for Blackbeard. In 1717 Blackbeard was finally stopped and was killed in a battle with the British Navy off the coast of South Carolina.[6]

James Oglethorpe asked the king for a charter to form a colony between the Spanish-held land of what is now known as Florida and the English colony of South Carolina. The king granted a charter to Oglethorpe and his board of trustees for twenty-one years. They were given the land between the Savannah and the Altamaha rivers. The colony was named Georgia after King George II who had granted the charter.

Oglethorpe's idea in founding the colony was to allow the poor to start a new life and to offer a refuge to the people who were suffering religious persecution in England and Europe, as well as to establish a military barrier between Spanish-Florida and the English colonies of North and South Carolina. Settlers were promised free passage and fifty acres of land if they immigrated to Georgia. James Oglethorpe and his trustees chose thirty-five families from those they interviewed to be colonists in Georgia. In the spring of 1733, he and his colonists sailed from England with those they believed deserved a second change and indicated their willingness to work hard. Oglethorpe chose a high bluff over the Savannah River, which he felt could be defended from attack, to establish his colony. They named their settlement Savannah.

One of the first projects of the new colony was to establish a public garden. This garden attempted to grow different products to see what might be successfully grown in Georgia for export to England.

The original idea for products to be grown in Georgia was the growing of wine grapes. The growing of silk worms was another possibility, as silk was a very expensive fabric that was being imported into England and was therefore costly for the English nobles to purchase. If it could be grown in the colonies and exported to England, it would prove profitable for the English treasury. Silk worms imported from China eat mulberry leaves, so hundreds of mulberry trees were planted as food for the silk worms. If these crops were successful, it would have brought instant financial success to the colony. Unfortunately, the climate did not prove suitable to the growing of grapes or the production of silk worms, and some of the Georgia settlers began to move to the more settled colonies of North and South Carolina.

Oglethorpe began to search for other settlers. In 1734 Protestant (Lutheran) refugees from Salzburg, Austria, arrived and formed the settlement named Ebenezer, which was located upriver from Savannah. The colony of Ebenezer was very successful, and more German-speaking peoples were recruited to settle in Ebenezer.

Also to come were Scottish settlers from the Highlands of Scotland; they founded the town of New Inverness on the Altamaha River. This town was later renamed Darien. These settlers were fierce warriors and considered rather uncivilized by the more refined English settlers. The Scottish were settled in the land closest to the Spanish border, because the Spanish were ruthless fighters, and the English felt the Scottish warriors would keep the Spanish from trying to take over the land of the colony of Georgia. .

Georgia was the only colony to receive financial aid by a vote of Parliament. It was also the only colony to prohibit the importing of intoxicating liquor. At the time of the founding of the colony, it was to have no slaves. As an inducement to settle in Georgia, the colonists were to have their land free of rent for ten years, but they had no say in the government of the colony. At the end of the twenty-one years of the charter, the colony was to become a Royal Colony and be governed by the Crown.

Because of the restrictions on settlement there, the colony grew slowly. The settlers wanted to have rum; they wanted slaves to work their rice fields; and they wanted to be able to have a say in governing themselves. Another problem they faced was that the oldest son in the family was the only one who could inherit the land of their small farms; this practice was called *primogeni-*

ture. This was the same situation in England, and because of this practice many of the settlers who came to the colonies were the second, third, or fourth sons in the family—those who could not inherit the land (in England) upon their fathers' death.

The Spanish, with their capital in St. Augustine Florida, grew jealous of the growth of the Georgia Colony and tried to regain control over the land of Georgia. The Spanish attempted to get the Creek Indians to turn against the colonists but with little success. In the meantime, Oglethorpe took a number of the Scottish Highlanders, who were feared by the Spanish, and established a fort (Frederica) on Simons' Island. From there he sailed up Altamaha Sound and met other Scottish Highlanders and formed another fort there. He then moved to form a fort (St. Andrew's) on Cumberland Island. Next he moved to on to form Fort St. George, which would protect the mouth of St. John's River. The fort in Augusta was formed last. It was located far up the Savannah River to protect the settlers from Indian attacks. Both the French and the Spanish traders in the area had stirred up the Indians, and there were Indian attacks against the settlers.

The Spanish were not happy about the preparations for a strong defense of the colony. The Spanish detained Oglethorpe's messenger and threatened war. There were several tribes of friendly Indians in the area who came to offer aid to the colonists. The governor of St. Augustine decided to sign a peace treaty with the colony, but the governor in Spain would not approve the peace treaty. To solve the problem, a conference was called at Frederica. The Spanish demanded the return of all lands in South Carolina and Georgia below the parallel of Port Royal. The conference ended without an agreement.

Oglethorpe hurried back to England to raise troops to protect his colony. He arrived back in the colony in 1738 with the added troops. By this time Spain had reinforced St. Augustine.

Oglethorpe led a strike on Florida with six hundred regular troops, four hundred Carolina Militia, and a large body of friendly Indians. He surrounded St Augustine but didn't have any cannons to knock down the walls of the city, and Oglethorpe had to abandon his mission into Florida.

In the meantime, the Spanish sent a fleet of thirty-six ships from their base in Cuba; they entered the harbor of St. Simons in July 1742. Oglethorpe was greatly outnumbered, and because additional men from Carolina had not arrived he had to retreat and withdrew his troops to Frederica. He decided to stand his ground there and made a night attack upon the Spanish encampment at St. Simons. A Frenchman with the group of colonists deserted to the enemy, and Oglethorpe again was forced to withdraw.

Oglethorpe designed a plan not only to punish the Frenchman who deserted, but also to scare the Spanish. Oglethorpe sent a letter to the Frenchman making it appear the Frenchman had deserted on purpose to serve as a spy for the colonists. In the letter he asked the supposed spy to tell the Spanish what a weak band of soldiers were with Oglethorpe and that they should attack the colonists immediately because within three days a fleet of British ships with two thousand soldiers would arrive to attack St. Augustine.

The Spanish believed the rouse and the Frenchman was hanged as a spy. When the Spanish spotted some ships coming from Carolina, they thought it was the arrival of the British troops, and Spain decided to attack the colonists immediately, defeat them, and then hurry back to protect St. Augustine from the supposed British troops on the approaching ships. The Spanish marched toward Frederica and were ambushed by Oglethorpe and his Scottish troops. They killed almost all of the Spanish invaders, and the colony was saved.

Oglethorpe returned to England in 1743 and died there at

the age of ninety. The colony enjoyed peace with its neighbors from then on. In 1749 Parliament made the change and allowed Georgia to become a slave colony. The laws of the colony were relaxed, and slaves were brought to Georgia from South Carolina. Later slave ships from Africa were allowed to dock in Savannah. With the introduction of slaves to do the work, the colony became prosperous.

In 1752 when the Charter expired, the colony was turned over to the king. It became a royal colony, and the people now were able to elect an assembly as their government, but the king appointed the governor. All Protestant freemen were allowed to vote. With the change in government, Georgia grew rapidly. The English church was still the official church, but it tolerated the practice of other Protestant religions; the Catholic religion still was not recognized, and the men who practiced Catholicism were not allowed to vote. The chief products were rice, lumber, and indigo (a blue dye), and they also carried on a fur trade with the Indians.

Afterword

This is the story of the founding of the thirteen colonies that formed the beginning of our country. Although the colonies were British colonies, men and women from many other countries came to each of the thirteen colonies. Some who came were fleeing from religious persecution; others just wanted an opportunity to better their lives in ways that were not possible in the countries from which they immigrated.

Imagine what it must have been like for men and women to leave the known world and move to the wilderness, facing all kinds of dangerous conditions just for the chance that they could provide a better life for themselves and their children. It would be similar to us taking a rocket ship and forming a colony on Mars or the moon, but without the use of cell phones or any way of easily communicating with those of us on the earth and without any modern equipment to make life easier. I don't know how many of us would be willing to make that journey.

(Endnotes)

1   Pobst, Sandra, *Voices from Colonial America*, National Geographic Society, Washington, D.C. 2005, 24–25.

2   Rosen, Daniel, *New Beginnings Jamestown and the Virginia Colony*, 1607–1699, National Geographic Society, Washington, D.C. 2005, 10.

3   iii Ibid Pobst, 45–46.

4   Greene, Meg, *Slave Young, Slave Long, The American Slave Experience*, Lerner Publications Company, Minneapolis, 1999, 7–9.

5   Winslow, Ola E., *Master Roger Williams*, Macmillan Company, New York, 1957, 137–138.

6   Pascal, Jeremy, *Pirates and Privateers*, Morristown, New Jersey, Silver Burdett press, 1981–1982, 24–29.

Appendix

English Kings and Queens during the Colonial and Revolutionary War Period in Order of Succession:

Elizabeth I: 1558–1603

James I: 1603–1625

Charles I: 1625–1649

Commonwealth period: 1649–1660

Charles II: 1660–1668

James II: 1668–1688

William & Mary: 1668–1702

Anne: 1702–1714

George I: 1714–1727

George II: 1727–1760

George III: 1760–1820 (the king during our Revolutionary War)